# Shoes

## The Sound of SH

By Peg Ballard

Shelly needed
new shoes.

3

# Mom took Shelly shopping.

4

# SHOES

5

# Shelly saw many shoes.

She saw
blue shoes.

9

10

She saw
pink shoes.

11

She saw
green shoes.

13

14

She saw
brown shoes.

She saw
shiny shoes.

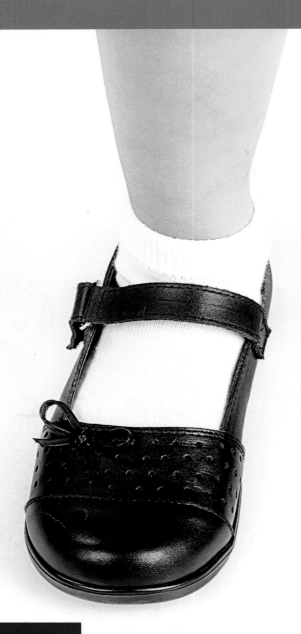
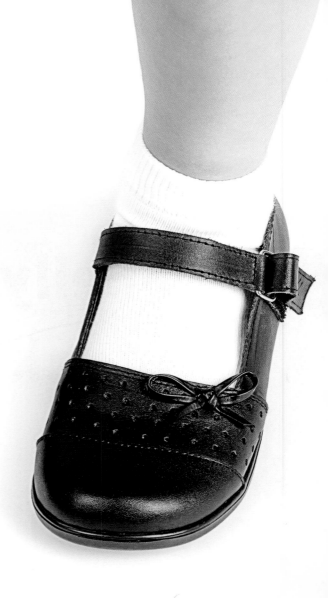

Shelly picked black shoes.

Shelly showed off her new shoes.

21

# Word List:

| | |
|---|---|
| she | shoes |
| Shelly | shopping |
| shiny | showed |

# Note to Parents and Educators

The books in this series are based on current research, which supports the idea that our brains are pattern-detectors rather than rules-appliers. This means children learn to read easier when they are taught the familiar spelling patterns found in English. As children encounter more complex words, they have greater success in figuring out these words by using the spelling patterns.

Throughout the series, the texts allow the reader to practice and apply knowledge of the sounds in natural language. The books introduce sounds using familiar onsets and *rimes*, or spelling patterns, for reinforcement.

For example, the word *cat* might be used to present the short "a" sound, with the letter *c* being the onset and "_at" being the rime. This approach provides practice and reinforcement of the short "a" sound, as there are many familiar words made with the "_at" rime.

The stories and accompanying photographs in this series are based on time-honored concepts in children's literature: well-written, engaging texts and colorful, high-quality photographs combine to produce books that children want to read again and again.

Dr. Peg Ballard
Minnesota State University, Mankato

**The Child's World®**
childsworld.com

Published by The Child's World®
1980 Lookout Drive • Mankato, MN 56003-1705
800-599-READ • www.childsworld.com

**PHOTO CREDITS**
© arapix/Shutterstock.com: 18, 21; cynoclub/Shutterstock.com: 14; Daniel M. Silva/Shutterstock.com: 5; Dmitri Ma/Shutterstock.com: 6; Everything/Shutterstock.com: 10; Family Business/Shutterstock.com: cover, 9; marekuliasz/Shutterstock.com: 13; photographyfirm/Shutterstock.com: 17; Sara Borbala Balogh/Shutterstock.com: 2

ISBN 9781503819290
LCCN 2016960520

Printed in the United States of America
PA02337

**ABOUT THE AUTHOR**

Dr. Peg Ballard holds a PhD from Purdue University and is an associate professor in the Department of Elementary & Early Childhood Education at Minnesota State University, Mankato. Her areas of expertise are assessment, interventions, and response to intervention. Dr. Ballard teaches online graduate courses in the K–12 reading licensure and master's program along with reading interventions in the undergraduate teacher preparation program.